REFLECTIONS FOR THE FUTURE

Reflections on my life and life lessons

By

Bobby Varghese

Table of Contents

PART 1: Reflections of my career

Chapter I: Advice I wish I had as a fresher.
Chapter II: If I were 22: What would I do differently?
Chapter III: Leadership - Rowing across cultures
Chapter IV: Transportation- The next level!
Chapter V: Good and Popular versus Good and Unpopular!
Chapter VI: The Leadership Square: Where do we fit in?

PART 2: Reflections of my life

Chapter I: The joy of nature!
Chapter II: The Ant - an unconventional Teacher
Chapter III: The Good Samaritan
Chapter IV: When I was 15 – Bobby
Chapter V: Failure: A true step towards learning!
Chapter VI: The dark of knight rises: The leap faith
Chapter VII: Imagine the unimaginable!
Chapter VIII: One in Seven Billion!
Chapter IX: Petrichor!

PART 1: Reflections of my career

Chapter I: Advice I wish I had as a fresher

Recently, one of my close friends sent me the CV of his son and asked me to assist him to get a suitable opportunity in the industry.

This set me thinking of my days as a freshly qualified chartered accountant who arrived in Mumbai seeking employment. I have to admit that this is one of the most difficult times in a person's career, especially if you do not have any mentors or contacts within the industry who can help you. I remember catching the train every day at 11 am (to avoid the Mumbai trains rush hour) from Kurla, a suburb in Mumbai to Victoria terminals for my daily job hunt. I would seek out one large skyscraper each day and then look at the name plates of the companies housed within and start approaching them with my CV one by one. Most of the time I could not even get past the security guard, who would politely take a copy of the CV and ask me to leave. Those were tough times and it took me over two months to land my first job. God was good to me and I also had some advice from some good people along the way and it has been a long journey since.

When I look at all the freshly graduated youngsters who come to new cities seeking job opportunities, I cannot help but share with them some of the advice which I wish I had when I was in their shoes. Here goes:

1. **Have faith**:

This is the most important step in the job-hunting process. Some of you may not have faith in God, but in my personal experience this really works. I remember having lost the chance to work with Arthur Andersen when I arrived in Mumbai, which in hind sight was a divine intervention to lead me in the right track. If I had got the role with Arthur Andersen, I would have soon lost my job with the closure of the firm. There are several instances in my future career I can quote, which has helped me to choose the right career option at the right time and realize that failures are there for a purpose.

2. Never give up:

This sounds very clichéd but this is another important aspect of being a fresh job hunter. There would be several rejections you will have to face day in and day out but never let your faith in God and yourself be lost. Remember that there will be point in time, when that special company which will launch your career will come around. You need to be there to grab it when the time comes. I remember that there were instances when I would come to the last level of the interview and then they would say, "Sorry, we picked a more experienced candidate". I wanted to yell, "How do I get experience if none of you will give me a chance?". But keep at it and you will win in the end.

3. Buy a lottery ticket:

No, I do not mean "go ahead and buy a lottery ticket.". What I mean is God helps only those who help themselves. If you want to get that dream job and you sit at home and pray all day with no efforts from your side, you will not get any job. If you want to win the lottery, the first step is to buy the lottery ticket. You have to put in the efforts first. Let no one fool you to say that getting the first job is a walk in the park. It may be for some, who are well connected but the feeling of getting the first job on your own steam lends itself a different kind of satisfaction. So, go ahead and buy the lottery ticket!

4. Look for learning opportunities:

When you get a chance to choose between position and money versus a fantastic learning opportunity, choose the latter. It is very important that you learn the ropes and be really good at what you do at the beginning of your career. Work hard and excel in your field. Money and promotions will follow you. This also means that choose to work with a good leader, someone who is a role model. The initial phase of your career is very important to establish your work ethics, technical skills and professionalism which will define your future career.

5. Learn to respect:

The greatness of a leader lies in his humility and his ability to respect people at all levels. During my job-hunting days, I came across many personalities who would disrespect you because they have the power to do so. You will learn later on that respect is commanded and not demanded. Learn to respect all whom you meet along the way, the tea boy, the receptionist and all the way upto the CEO. You never know who among them would be the one who would return the favor.

6. Ethics:

Never compromise on your ethics. There will be many instances where you will be tempted to do something wrong or look the other way. This is very easy to do but the most important legacy you can leave behind is your values and ethics you have brought into each role that you handled. I have faced this situation many times in my career and have felt afraid several times that I could lose my job. But truth has always prevailed in the end and I do not remember a single day when I went to sleep at night, without a clear conscience. God has been good and I also had support from the senior leadership.

7. People management:

What I have realized now that most of the technical knowledge that I gained from my school and professional studies are hardly used as I advance in my career. What is sought after are team building skills, stakeholder management, drive and passion to obtain results. That does not mean that professional qualifications are not important. If I were not a Chartered Accountant, I would not have got many of the positions that I have worked in but this is only a stepping stone in your career. Years later people remember you for the good deeds you have done for them, the kindness you have shown to them and the results they have achieved through your motivation and not really your technical qualifications.

To close, I can say that I have by no means reached the pinnacle of my career and technical abilities. I am still learning each day and making mistakes. It has been fun though and I have made some good friends along the way. If the above advice would help some of you who are starting their job search, I would be a happy person.

Chapter II: If I were 22: What would I do differently?

At the outset, let me say that I am firm believer in God and the divine plan that he has for our life. I am thankful to him for the ways in which he has led me. There have been many ups and downs and when I look back I have realised that all the difficulties that I have gone through was for a reason, which in most cases I have realised later on. I thank God for the ways in which he continues to lead us as a family.

If I look back on my career and think what I would have done differently, if I were 22 again, a few things pop up to my mind:

1. I would have trusted God more and worried less:

As the Bible says in "[1 Corinthians 10:13](#) - There hath no temptation taken you but such as is common to man: but God is faithful, who will not suffer you to be tempted above that ye are able; but will with the temptation also make a way to escape, that ye may be able to bear it]". Having seen the mighty deeds of God in my life, I would have learnt that I should worry less when I face problems and know that things would work out for the best in the end.

2. Learn a foreign language:

I am currently working in the Middle East and I have come across many job advertisements for good positions which I could not apply for, although I had all the qualifications and experience just because Arabic was a requirement and I did not know it. I would recommend all youngsters to learn at least one international language, either Arabic, Spanish, French, German or Chinese before you start working. The difference it makes in your career, if you are working in a different country and you can speak the local language is truly great!

3. **Do not mix insurance with investment:**

As soon as you start earning, there will be a host of insurance agents who would try and sell you insurance policies which have also some saving scheme attached to it. Before you buy this, let me tell you, do not go for it. Buy a term plan for your insurance which will have a cheaper premium and use other avenues for investments. The policies I have taken when I was 22 have high premiums, low coverage, long tenures and poor returns. On top of it, I cannot surrender these policies without a substantial loss.

4. **Start saving early**:

I need not emphasis the power of compounding on your savings. Someone who has started saving early, would have a greater corpus towards the end of his career. Of course, this is not easy to implement since there will always be temptations like the latest mobile phone, clothes, watches and the list goes on. Man is never satisfied. When you buy a Casio watch you will aim to then own a Tissot watch. When you own a Tissot watch, you will aim to own a Patek Phillipe. At the end of the day, these are all watches and it is the ego and eternal dissatisfaction of human nature that prods us to keep going on and on.

5. **Select a popular industry**:

In my rush to land my first role, I jumped into an industry which does not have a wide scope and I got typecast. I kept growing in my role within the logistics industry but as a result, I have found it difficult to take up a similar role in finance in another industry. So, I would say to all those 22-year olds, choose an industry which has a great scope for flexibility like manufacturing, FMCG, Banking etc

Having said this, each of us has a purpose in life and it does serve us to worry away our life! It is good to be alive and thank God for the gift of life!

Chapter III: Leadership - Rowing across cultures

I have been working in the Middle East since 2011, a short time compared to many expatriates. It is very common to see expatriates who have spent close to 30 years or more in the Middle East. I spent around 13 years of my career in India and then moved to the Middle East working across Oman, Saudi Arabia and now the UAE.

There are times when I sit and reflect how in the world did, I manage to reach this far. I currently lead a team of around 40 staff, from various cultures and countries. Each day is a new learning experience and each interaction with my team members is an opportunity to learn, inspire, be inspired and jointly working towards achieving a common goal. I would like to share with you some of the insights and learning from my career on managing a multi-cultural workforce. I am in no means an expert but I have failed many times in my journey here and I hope that some of you can avoid the mistakes I made.

After 6 years of working in Mumbai as a senior manager and leading a small team, I was selected for a global leadership program. I was excited since this was a unique program which included only a select few participants from several countries across the world. The group was a mixed set of professionals from USA, Europe, China, Thailand, India, Malaysia, Africa and Russia. The program was a two-year management course with 4 two-week on-site training in four different countries. The first segment of the program was held in Holland and Denmark, with a one-week boot camp program in the forested area of Denmark.

The boot camp program changed my perspective on global leadership completely. As part of the boot camp, we were grouped into teams of 10-12 persons and I was put in charge of a multi-cultural group. The teams were given a mission to complete, where we had to compete against each other to rescue a ship wrecked passenger from a ship that had sunk close to the shore. There were Chinese, American, British, Russian and Danish to name a few nationalities in the team. After a day in the field with the team, my team would not listen to me, they had internally chosen a different leader and we did not win the contest.

I was extremely disappointed and all my self-esteem had spiraled downwards. The boot camp left a lasting impression on me and let me learn some very hard truths about leadership across cultures. While I was in India, my team would listen to every word I said and we could achieve the tasks we set out to do. I kept thinking why did this approach not work when I had a team of people from different countries? Thankfully, we had experienced mentors on the program with us who could reflect on my actions and give me some insight on where I could improve. We could bounce off our thoughts and concerns with these well experienced mentors from the industry real time, which made the learning more practical.

Here are some of the learning from my boot camp experience in the Danish jungles:

1. **Realize that people are people:**

At first, when I took charge of the team with people from different countries, I was confused. Each person looked different, spoke English differently, had different values and responded differently. Having spent time with them for a full day, I realised that in the end, all of them are people with the same feelings, aspirations, goals and nature. They may look different and have different mannerisms which may be reflective of the country they were from but in the end, they are human beings just like you and me. They recognize leadership traits irrespective of the country you are from. This is why we see Global MNCs led by people from different countries. It does not matter which part of the world you are from, leadership qualities are recognized and respected equally the world over.

2. Be there for the team:

One of the parts of the mission was for each team member to carry different parts of a stretcher across a few kilometers of sandy beach. Once we reached the final destination, we were supposed to assemble the stretcher as a team. Some of us had lighter components and moved ahead of the group and there were a few who lagged behind who were carrying the heavy logs for the stretcher. A few of us reached the final spot early and started resting. It took almost half an hour for the rest of the team to reach and they were pretty angry to see us resting. In hindsight, I realized that once I had reached the final spot, I should have gone back to help the lagging team members. This is what leadership is about. To have a genuine concern for the team and to pull them through difficulties. You have to do the tasks assigned to you and also help your team members with theirs.

3. Give clear instructions:

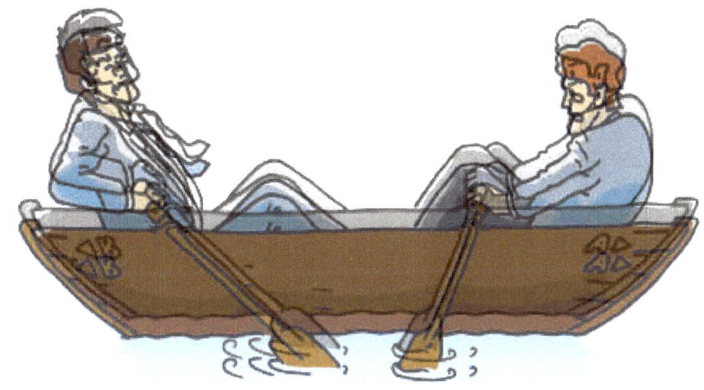

Another part of the mission was to carry the stranded woman on the stretcher and row a paddle boat across the ocean for around six kilometers. Our boat did not move for quite some time in spite of us all rowing very hard. Each of us were rowing in a different direction and due to the different groups, that had been formed within the team, they were not listening to me.

It is important to build trust early on with the team members and let them know that they can depend on you and you know your job. They will respect you then and will follow directions to achieve the common goal.

4. **A leader must know when to serve**:

One of the hindrances during our team program was that I was always trying to take the driver's seat as a leader. Irrespective of my skill level in a particular task, I tried to pretend that I knew what I was doing and tried to give directions to the team. This is a mistake. They can easily understand that you are not aware and will call your bluff. There is no shame in admitting to the team that you do not know something and giving the reins to another team member to lead a particular task, even though you are the leader by title. The team will respect your humility and will be inspired to work together and contribute positively.

5. **Give Respect to be respected**:

Whichever country and culture you belong to, bad manners are never appreciated. I quickly learnt that team members genuinely respect you if you give them respect. For example, we had a Chinese person who was very quiet most of the time and there were others in the team who made fun of him. During one of our class room sessions, we learnt that he had the sharpest IQ in solving logical questions way before all of us and the reason he was quiet earlier was because he was not very good at speaking English and he felt that the others would tease him. Each person is talented in his own way and it is the leader's job to find out the talent and put it to use. We need people with different skill sets and talent to build a powerful winning team. People will come forward if you respect them.

6. **Smile- The Universal language**:

Finally, there is one language which every person from every country understands and that is the language of the smile. The picture says it all. A smile builds a bond quickly within the team. Smile often and be patient and tolerant with the other team members.

Over the two years of the program, there was much more learning and opportunity to correct my mistakes. We all grew together as a group and when I graduated, my colleagues in the group and my tutors voted me as one of the "Best graduates" for that year. All of us grew as leaders during this program and I am no better than any of them. I thank them especially, for the tolerance and goodwill they showed towards me, during our time together. We are good friends even to this day and I feel confident to pick up the phone and speak to them, if I need be, whichever part of the world they are in.

Chapter IV: Transportation- The next level

We live in a time where the means of transport is so advanced that we love to travel. It is easy and comfortable to move from one place to another, from one country to another and even into space. This was not so easy a few decades back. We can only imagine a time before the first automated car was invented by Karl Benz in the year 1885.

Even not so long ago, my parents have told me stories of how people living in the villages in India used to walk miles and miles a few decades back. Even today there are places where there is no comfortable means of automated transportation.

This led me to think in spite of all the advancement in transportation, what does the future hold? What would the next level in transportation?

Here are a few secrets wishes that have crossed my mind several times, which I would like to share with you. I am sure many of you would have felt the same too.

1. During the peak hour of traffic, when your car is stuck in a traffic jam, have we not wished our car could fly and none of the rest could? We could take off and fly away in style when all the other cars were stranded in traffic!
2. We think we have bought all the documents required to get our paperwork done at the bank and the bankers says that they need that one piece of paper which we left home thinking it was not needed. How we wish we could disappear and appear at our homes and be back with that vital piece of paper in a few seconds!
3. We cherish our childhood memories and all the past years in our life. There are many times we think if we could have travelled back in time to do things differently! That's time travel for you.
4. We see the birds fly and the fish swim without the aid of any mechanical equipment. Imagine if we could do the same. If all men had these abilities but did not know how to harness them till now?
5. We are all fascinated by outer space and what lies in the vast unknown. If we could freely travel into space and back without having to use rockets worth billions of dollars?
6. If all our vehicles could run on their own without the need for air polluting fuel? If we invented a form of energy which does not pollute and does not require manual refueling?
7. If our cars could be such that it could be designed to drive on the road, fly in the air and dive underneath the water?
8. If there was a way to instantly communicate with other cars on the road to tell them, "Hey, your door is open" or "Give way, my friend, I need to get ahead of you".
9. If sea transport was faster and more efficient than Air travel to ensure that all goods are transported only by sea! This would be a big win for the Maritime trade.
10. And the craziest thought of all, if we could be present physically or mentally at more than one place at the same time!

Who knows that these steps in transportation may be realized at some point in future! Until then, lets learn to be patient while we are stuck in the traffic jam! Thank God for inventing Music🎵🎶 to pass the time during rush hour.

Have we reached the pinnacle of transportation capabilities or is it just the beginning?

Chapter V: Good and Popular versus Good and Unpopular!

I still recall the mail that I received from my first boss, "Do you want to be good and popular or good and unpopular?". There is a big difference between the two.

It was the second year of my working life in the industry and I was employed as an Assistant Manager in the Mumbai branch of the company. I was in a hurry to do things, wanted to do everything yesterday and was highly impatient. I could not tolerate slow learners and people with low I Q. I was good at my job and learnt things very quickly but slowly I started making enemies since I was impatient with people. Being young, I thought I was doing my work very well and improving in my career. At one point in time, I was having an email exchange with a customer service staff who was not willing to help me. Being in Finance, I needed some information which I demanded be sent immediately.

This is when my boss stepped in said, why don't you meet the person and explain your problem, request his help and really listen to him. I tried it for a lark and guess what...it worked! This is when I realised that true success in your role is being good at what you do and also being popular with your colleagues. It does not mean compromising on your values and integrity but being firm in your beliefs and assertive. At the same time, it implies being tactful and empathetic while dealing with your colleagues.

You may be a genius at your work but if you are not able to manage your stakeholders, then you are not truly successful. Many leaders try to demand respect and forget the fact that true respect is commanded and not demanded.

I have practiced patience since then and am still learning this skill. I have a lot of friends at my workplace now but I still do not compromise on my beliefs and integrity.

It is harder to be Good and Popular than Good and Unpopular!

Chapter VI: The Leadership Square: Where do we fit in?

There must be umpteen books and articles written about leadership and it is quite normal for someone to wonder if there is anything new written here. It is of course up to the reader to decide after reading what I have to say. "The Leadership Square" is one of my fundamental principles of identifying what sort of a leader a person is:

To begin with, I call it the Leadership square because it represents the four important stakeholders that every leader has to manage, inspire and lead in the course of their daily life. The following is a description of the four sides of the leadership square:

1. The lower side of the square: Leaders team members:

The lower side of the square represents the leaders team members. The team members are represented on the lower side since the team members are managed directly by the leader and report to the latter. There are many leaders who are not able to adequately manage their team members. An empathy for the team and an inspirational leadership style is required to lead the team members.

2. The Upper side of the square: Leader's Superiors:

The upper side of the square represents the leader's relationship with his superiors. There are many leaders who are very good at managing teams but they are not good at managing upwards. I remember one of my bosses telling me early on in my career that, "It is important to do a good job and also to show that you are doing a good job". You need to be your self-advocate and learn to play the positive politics to promote yourself and your career. This should not be however, at the expense of your team members or peers. For as they say, when you fall, they are the ones below and beside the corporate ladder who will break your fall.

3. **The right side of the square: Leader's peers**:

The right side of the square represents the leader's peers. It could be other department heads, CEOs of other business units etc, depending on which position the leader is in. The success of a leader is also dependent on what his peers think of him or her. Many times, a part of the leader's appraisal is about asking his peers on how he is doing. This is where networking with your peers, giving them the due respect and generally taking time to give them a call when you do not need anything makes a lot of difference in building a good relationship with your peers. And yes, my definition of networking is calling on and meeting up with your contacts when you do not need anything from them. This way, they will help you when you really need something.

4. **The left side of the square: Leader's stakeholders**:

The left side of the square represents all the other stakeholders affecting the leader's role like Board members, investors, suppliers, customers, government agencies and other external and internal stakeholders. Many leaders do not pay attention to this side of the square and spend more time managing upwards or downwards in the square.

You may be wondering now what is the meaning of all the four sides of the leadership square? Well, good question?

As mentioned earlier, the four sides of the square represent the four important stakeholders a leader needs to manage to be truly successful. In your daily life, if you place the square on any real-life leader you can see how well he or she is performing. A true leader is one who is able to manage all four sides of the square successfully. Based on the leadership square, there are three types of leaders we can see in our daily life:

a. **The dysfunctional Leader**:

These are the leaders who are able to successfully manage only one side of the square. He could be good at managing teams (lower side) but very poor at managing the perceptions of his superiors. Such leaders may be loved by their teams but many not go very far up in the corporate ladder.

There are also leaders who are able to successfully manage the upper side of the square, i.e. manage the perceptions of his bosses but very poor at managing his team. Such leaders are also commonly seen in every organisation, although you may have to look deep to identify them. They tend to move very quickly up the corporate ladder but will hit a dead end soon when they meet a smart boss who is able to pull his bluff. Perhaps, an exception is the army where such people lead due to their position and not by inspiration.

In general, these leaders attain short term success but will never be remembered in the long term as someone who really made a difference. It would be better for such persons to remain as individual contributors or Managers.

b. **The average leader:**

Many of the leaders we see in our day to day life fall in this category and continue to be there since they are successful in managing more than one side of the square. This is the state most leaders are in and this is not a bad state to be in. Leadership is a continuous journey, where we are each day learning to deal with and excel at managing all four sides of the square. These leaders are able to run organisations, teams and groups. People do not mind having them around but may not be remembered as exceptional leaders if they do not grow to the next level.

c. **The inspirational leader**:

It is very rare to meet such a leader and you will instantly recognise him when you start dealing with him. He will be able to talk with equal ease to the lowest level of staff to the highest level in the organisation. He has a personal charisma which will allow him to influence all four sides of the square successfully. These leaders have genuine empathy for people and are result oriented, bold and passionate in what they do.

In summary, all of us are on a leadership journey and are struggling each day to manage all the four sides of the square. It is important to identify which stage of leadership we are in and which side of the leadership square needs to be improved. Some people achieve this early, some late and some may never be an inspirational leader at all in their career.

Ask yourself the question where do you fit in the leadership square. Whichever stage you are in your leadership journey, keep trying and improving your skills. There will be a day when you will be recognised if you really strive hard.

PART II: Reflections of my life

Chapter I: The joy of nature!

Over the last three years we have moved across three countries, Oman, Saudi Arabia and now Abu Dhabi in the UAE. If I look back, these three years have been a whiz of activity and continuous work. One of the downsides of these inter country movements, other than the nightmare of packing and repacking our things and shifting houses and schools (this is my wife's main concern!) is the fact that we did not get to take a real holiday in between. Each time we moved from one country to the other, I had to join the new job immediately after leaving the previous one. Upon joining, there was then the issue of settling down, visas, schools, housing, transportation and finally the probation period. Any expat will find this familiar ground and I sympathize with my fellow expats.

During March 2015, I decided to take a week off and stay at home. My first real break after a long time! Normally, we took breaks to travel to India or go on an overseas vacation. This was new to me and the thought of sitting at home not doing anything was not very welcoming.

Abu Dhabi is a beautiful city and this is the city where I grew up and did my schooling. It was almost 25 years ago that I left Abu Dhabi as a student and now I was back as an employee. The Abu Dhabi of now has changed so much for the better and we as a family love the place! One of my colleagues referred to Abu Dhabi as a "hidden gem" and I totally agree. You are reluctant to visit Abu Dhabi at first but then once you have visited then you don't need to be convinced for the next time! This is a cosmopolitan city which is safe, secure and family friendly.

Oops! Now my post is sounding like an Ad for Abu Dhabi city! Coming back to the topic, I decided that during my one-week holiday, I would visit some of the famous parks in Abu Dhabi. I love nature and some of my earliest memories as a child are chasing butterflies in my home town in Kerala. Sitting down on the grass and looking at the sky and counting the stars. Looking at how green were the leaves of the trees and how wonderfully God had created nature. Over the years since I started working, I have hardly looked at nature or spent time admiring its beauty. Parks and greenery have been part of the scenery which I passed by on my day to work. I discovered that there was a line of parks on the corniche road in Abu Dhabi with several beautiful parks one after the other, Lake Park, Family Park etc. One morning I went to the Lake Park and really felt blessed. I just sat there on the grass and the park benches smelling the fresh clean air, hearing the sound of birds and watching the butterflies. It reminded me of my childhood and the wonder of God's creation. I felt rejuvenated. And I realized that you do not need to travel all the way to an exotic location to feel good. The joy of nature is one which you can enjoy if we stop for a short while in our daily rat race and take a break! Thereafter, I took my family to these parks and they loved it. These parks are also one of the favorite spots for my wife and daughter. We took one of our family friends who has been living in Abu Dhabi for the last 9 years and they were amazed that there were such facilities in this city. They had been here for the last 9 years but had never visited these parks and I am sure it must be the case with many of the residents here.

The last week we visited another beautiful park in Abu Dhabi, the Mushrif Park (pictured above), which is also brilliant made. It is really awesome to see money well spent on making and maintaining these parks in the middle of the concrete jungle.

May I ask my friends and colleagues to try this experience of being one with nature for a short while! To see the difference, it makes in our lives!

The joy of nature!

Chapter II: The Ant - an unconventional Teacher

Sitting peacefully on the ledge of my office window sill is the replica of an Ant, made from plastic. It has been there in my office for quite some time. Last week, one of my colleagues asked me the reason why I kept the Ant in my office and I thought it might be a good idea to share my thoughts on this.

No, I am not crazy and I do not worship the ant! It is only God I believe in and his mercy in our lives. The ant is there to remind me of some important lessons, which I do not want to lose focus of, as I rush through my daily work life.

All of us tend to look up to heroes, historical figures and living legends for lessons on how to get better. We are keen to learn the secrets of their success and closely follow their wise sayings. With social media nowadays, you can see a lot of such wise sayings on a daily basis liked by your friends. But we forget that sometimes the biggest lessons in life come from the most common place things or people around us.

Take ants for instance. Would you believe those small creatures can teach us how to live a better life? The Bible is a great teacher and the wisdom from the ants is referred in the following verses:

Proverbs 30:25 - The ants are a people not strong, yet they prepare their meat in the summer

Proverbs 6:6 - "Go to the ant, you sluggard; consider its ways and be wise."

When was the last time you saw ants reach an obstacle and give up with their heads down and head back to their ant hill to relax? Never. Imagine what you could accomplish if you never quit and always did all that you could do. Here are a few important lessons from the ants

1: Ants are well organized and disciplined

There are three types of ants in a colony, viz; workers, male and queen ants. Each of these types of ants serve a different purpose and they are well organised. They carry out all the tasks required to be done through division of labour. There are no traffic fines, penalties or court orders imposed on ants for not doing their jobs but still they religiously do so with discipline and organization. The lesson we can learn is to be disciplined and well organized in our life and success will follow.

2: Hardworking and strong

Ants keep themselves busy all day long. They are busy doing something all day long unlike some individuals who are busy doing nothing. While I am not saying that we must not rest, we must work hard during the working hours. You must have also seen that ants carry objects that are bigger than them. This is possible through hard work and determination. The learning is that if we do not focus on how big the task is and instead, give it our best we can accomplish what would seem to be an insurmountable task.

3: Persistent

If ants are headed somewhere and you try to stop them; they'll look for another way. They'll climb over, they'll climb under and they'll climb around. They keep looking for another way. We must never give up in the face of obstacles. No matter how hard the odds are, we must try out best to find a way to overcome them. Persistence, of course must be in pursuit of a worthwhile goal.

4: Teamwork

There is great sense of team work among the ants. Have you seen a set of ants fighting to do the same task? Each of them knows their roles in the colony and set about doing it with dedication and team work, helping each other out. If you watch carefully there is a co-ordination among the tasks done by the ants which result in reaching their larger goal like storing food or building colonies.

5. <u>Planning</u>

Ants are very good at planning than most people. They store up food during summer so that they can take care of themselves during winter, when food is scarce. They do not while away their time in foolish pursuits during summer.

The next time you see an ant or if you pass by my office and see the plastic ant, please think about what I said and the phenomenal lessons in life which such a small animal teaches us. It also shows that we can learn from anyone and everyone if we are observant and humble in our attitude.

Courage isn't always a lion's roar. It is also the silence of an ant working patiently, persistently and never giving up.

Never give up, look ahead, stay positive and do all you can.

Chapter III: The Good Samaritan

Last week I was driving from Abu Dhabi to Dubai on the fast lane. There were cars behind me at a safe distance and I was in a hurry to reach home. When I reached half way, I heard a loud noise from my rear tyres and my car started skidding. I assumed that one of the tyres had burst and tried to control the car. By the grace of God, none of the cars behind me slammed into my car and I was able to safely move my car to the service lane on the right side of the road.

When I got down and looked at my tyres, I found that they have not burst but the lining above the left tyre had come off and was flapping all over the tyre. I tried to tear off the lining but it was made of tough canvas type material and could not be torn with the hands. I then looked at the tools in my car to see if there were any sharp objects to tear the lining off. After several unfruitful attempts, I could not find any tools to tear off the lining.

I was standing on the side of the highway and watching all the other cars pass by. I wished someone would stop to help me. I had put the hazard lights on but everyone passed by without stopping. I thought of calling the break down service but I knew it would take a long time for them to come and I was in a hurry to reach home. Finally, I started driving the car slowly with the hazard lights flashing with the intent to reach the nearest petrol pump, where I hoped to find someone to help me.

Just as I was driving forward, a car stopped in front of me. The driver jumped out of the car and asked me to stop. He had a pocket knife in his hand and he came straight to the tyre and started cutting away the lining. He could not speak English and I assumed he was someone from an Arabic speaking nation. He was on the floor with dirtied hands and cut away the lining and made sure the car was in a driving condition. I could only thank this Good Samaritan who refused to accept anything other than a hand shake on his wrist since his hands were dirty. As I drove by, I saw him washing his hands and he smiled at me.

I thanked God that day for keeping me safe from a major accident and also for sending a Good Samaritan to help me on the highway. I could only but think back and be ashamed that I had passed the same highway many times and have seen people stopped on the service roads with their hazard lights flashing, wishing someone would stop and help them. I never paid attention and this may be the case with many of us who drive down this road of life. Let us stop by and help our fellow men, if they are in need. I hope that I will be able to be a good Samaritan to somebody in need of help one of these days!

Chapter IV: When I was 15 – Bobby

When I was 15, I wanted to be a professional soccer player!

I had been crazy about soccer since my childhood, playing the game with my friends whenever I could get some free time. The constant practice led me to be selected in the District level team in Kerala state of India. I was then sent to the Kerala State level selections! Each player was allowed 5 minutes to show off his skill in the selections. Before I went into the field, I asked the coach, "What happens if I get selected?". He said "You have to attend a two-month coaching camp". The camp coincided with my Xth standard Board exams. In my mind I thought of the best football player and his recognition in my country. I decided I would write my Board exams instead. I went into the field during my 5 minutes' worth of fame and just stood there doing nothing, afraid that I may get selected if I touch the ball. And now I am a chartered accountant! I love what I do now but I also wish for all the 15-year olds from India who love soccer to follow their dreams!

I wish that soccer would get the recognition it deserves and may be treated at the same level as cricket in India!

Chapter V: Failure: A true step towards learning!

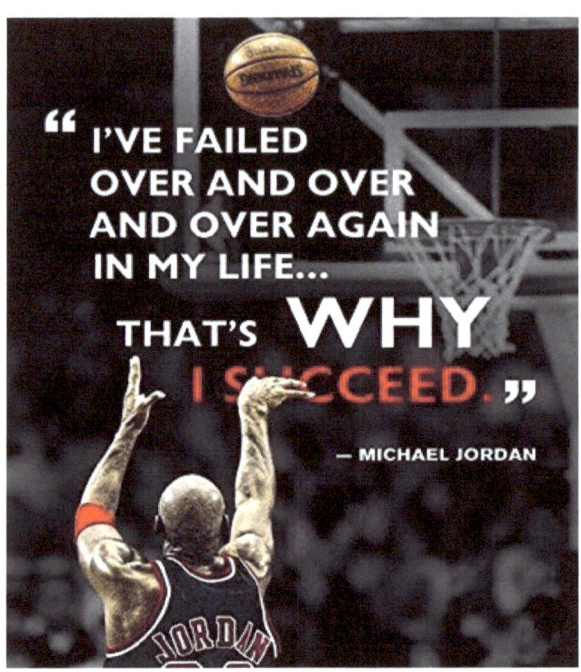

From a young age we are always tuned by our parents, friends, peers and society at large that it is all about winning. It is not good enough if you have not won and secured first place in every competition, every class and every situation in life. Does this sound all too familiar?

Well guess what? I believe it is all right to fail once in a while and we can never truly be successful if we have never failed in our lives. You must have read about great stories of King Bruce and the Spider, Abraham Lincoln and Thomas Alva Edison as to how many times they had failed in many endeavors in their lives before they became great and successful people. Their story teaches about perseverance amidst failure which we all know about and perseverance is not the subject here.

It is failure as a step to learning and success!

I remember the first time I faced my greatest failure. I had passed all the classes in school with good grades and even in college I managed to secure the sixth rank in the University, in spite of studying extremely hard for these exams. The first major failure took place when I was studying for my Chartered Accountancy (CA) exams. This is supposed to be one of the toughest exams in India and the remarkable thing about the course is that "it is extremely easy and cheap to enroll but extremely difficult to graduate from" unlike other courses like MBA. I passed my CA Intermediate exam in the first attempt and was very proud of myself. There were accolades all around from people since it was not very common for guys to pass when studying this course in

Kerala. Most people move to one of the metro cities in India to appear for this course. For the final exam, there were two parts and I earnestly studied for the exams. It also helped that I had gone to Chennai for a few months for tuitions for some of the tougher subjects and was confident of passing the exam. After three months of intensive studies, I wrote the exams and was confident of passing. When the results came, I was devastated. I has passed in the group which I did not take tuitions but had failed in the group in which I was very well prepared, by 3 marks.

This was really hard hitting and a turning point in my life. Suddenly, I was facing the first real failure in my life. Suddenly, all the accolades turned to jeers from the society, peers and every other smart alec who knew me. I could not understand why in spite of all my efforts, I had failed. I requested a recount of my answer sheet also but with no luck. It took me a while to get over this and I wrote again the next time and passed the CA Course.

The learnings from this major failure which I would like to share with you all are:

1. **Be Humble at all times**:

Success in life is a grace of God. You may have been blessed with a lot of abilities and this may give rise to a feeling that we are invincible and will succeed in everything that we do. This is not true. At the end, we need to remember that we are all human and we do fail at times. This means also that we need to be tolerant to our fellow human being's failures. As Psalms 118: 8 says "It is better to trust in the Lord than put confidence in man". Prepare well and work really hard to overcome the task on hand but put your faith in God to see you through.

I remember going for my driving test in Oman. After 10 years of driving in India, I thought the test would be a cake walk and told everyone so. I got my license in the third attempt after failing twice and I was humbled. It was the roundabouts and right side driving in Oman which needed getting used to. In Mumbai, we do not have roundabouts. If there was space for a roundabout, there would have been a building erected there by now. I had a whole new attitude towards the driving test in Abu Dhabi, where I live now and by the grace of God, I passed in the first attempt.

2. **We cannot please everyone at all times**:

People will say good things about you when you succeed and the same people will say bad things and abandon you when you fail. We cannot live our lives to please everyone. I keep asking myself sometimes, all the people who give me sage advice when I succeed; how many of them would be there to give me a hundred rupees, if I had become poor and asked them for it. Suddenly, the advice would vanish and so would they. Learn to live our life to be honest to ourselves and to God. Those who stand by you in times of trouble are your true friends. Failure is the sieve of friendship. You will know who your true friends are when you fail.

3. **There is always light at the end of the tunnel**:

This is perhaps cliché but true. Ever heard of these sayings:

"After every dusk, there is a dawn".

"It is darkest before dawn"

This is one of the greatest learnings from failure. Try, Try till you succeed. If once you fail, we should keep trying provided the task is something which is achievable. It is interesting to see a child learning to ride a bicycle. He may fall down 10 times but he always gets up and picks up the bicycle again and in the end he is riding it so well. This is the innocent faith of a child who does not accept failure.

I like this cartoon, which shows that many times we work so hard and fail and give up at the time, when if we had toiled a little longer, we would have seen great success!

To sum up, there is no true learning without failure and we cannot truly enjoy our success if we have not failed!

Chapter VI: The dark of knight rises: The leap faith

"There's a reason why this prison is the worst hell on earth... Hope. Every man who has rotted here over the centuries has looked up to the light and imagined climbing to freedom. So easy... So simple... And like shipwrecked men turning to sea water from uncontrollable thirst, many have died trying. I learned here that there can be no true despair without hope."—Bane

I recently saw a short clip of the "Pit scene" in the movie, The Dark knight rises. If you have not seen this, I recommend that you do.

The Pit is a prison located in the ancient part of the world, which had established such a fearsome reputation that it became referred to as "the worst Hell on Earth". The Pit also featured a well-like structure which the prisoners were free to climb in order to attempt their escape. Nearly everyone who tried the climb failed due to the gap between two ledges being too far to jump. The legend of the only person to ever escape (young Talia al Ghul) inspired Bruce Wayne to believe that escape was possible.

In this scene, Bruce has been thrown into the pit and he is down with a broken back. The scene is about how he overcomes his fear and attempts to climb out of the pit. Each time he tries to make the climb with a rope tied around his waist, he falls down. The most significant scene is when the older inmate tells Bruce Wayne the secret of how young Talia Al Ghul makes the jump. She jumped without the rope tied around her waist and she made it!!! Bruce does the same shortly and he is out of the pit.

If we relate this to real life, many times we do not succeed because we make halfhearted attempts, with a rope tied around our waist. When the fear that there is no rope around your waist is there, we give our very best to succeed and believe it or not, we do. At the same time, the task must be one which is achievable as in this case, there was a precedent of someone escaping the pit earlier.

This has really inspired me to believe that no matter how difficult your circumstances, have a strong faith in God and give your very best and achieve the impossible! Yes, Plan B is important but do not give it more importance than your Plan A.

Jump with all your might towards your goal. Remove the rope around your waist and your strong faith in God along with a clear realisation of the consequences of failure will propel you towards your goal!

Chapter VII: Imagine the unimaginable!

The Merriam-Webster Dictionary defines "imagination", as "the power of forming a mental image of something not present to the senses or never before wholly perceived in reality." I remember when we were kids, we used to tease a friend who used to say that he would only believe what he saw with his own eyes. Our conversation would go like this:

Me: "Do you have a brain?":

Friend: "Yes"

Me: "Have you seen your brain?"

Friend: "No"

Me: "Then how do you know if you have a brain, if you haven't seen it?"

Friend: <No answer>

It is not necessary that we must believe only those things that we can see with our own eyes or feel with our senses. There are many mysteries out there, which we cannot understand now with our limited imagination. The English poet William Blake described it more beautifully: "To see a World in a Grain of Sand and a Heaven in a Wild Flower, hold infinity in the palm of your hand and Eternity in an hour." If you see the strides humanity has taken in new technology and inventions in the last century, the list is innumerable. If you happen to see a documentary of the standard of living of people a few decades back, for example, a life without televisions, iPad, iPhone, vacuum cleaners, refrigerators, etc, many of us cannot even think of such a life.

If we watch science fiction movies, there are many concepts, like flying cars, laser beam guns, teleportation etc that we see and think in our minds "Unbelievable! These would never happen." To all those "nay Sayers", it is time to open our minds…..to imagine the Unimaginable! Just think about this, if we travel back in time and spoke to a person who was alive in the 18th century and told him that there would be a time when man would fly from one country to the other in aero planes, he would have the same reaction as what we have while watching the science fiction movies of today.

The human mind, I believe is a powerful tool, which the almighty God has gifted us. It is we as human being who create limitations by closing our minds to seemingly endless possibilities.

Let us now look at our current workplace. Have you noticed that managers who do not have an imaginative mind quash many ideas at the initial stage itself? The reasons could be many:

1. The new idea may involve additional work and efforts to be taken, which many managers and teams are averse to. They like the status quo.

2. The new idea is great but since it was not proposed by them in the first place, it would be better to shoot it down.
3. The person who proposed the new idea is too junior in the organisation to have any worthwhile idea.
4. I don't like the person who proposed this idea so I am not going to listen to what he says.
5. The manager has a limited imagination and cannot envisage the larger implications of the new idea.
6. Personality issues of the manager like "Not listening", "Busy with the phones during meetings", "Pride", etc.

Shooting down an idea without proper thought and consideration would be a missed opportunity. Good examples of this may be Sony Corporation ignoring the LCD Technology and Kodak missing the digital photo transition. Humans have come a long way from the inquisition of Galileo for stating that the earth is round. However, in spite of the dramatic leap in technology, subsequent years have demonstrated that when it comes to believing in one's potential, we are perennial doubters and nay Sayers.

I recently read in the newspaper that they are testing prototypes of flying cars! In the words of Robert F. Kennedy: "There are those who look at things the way they are, and ask 'why?'… I dream of things that never were, and ask 'why not?'". While humanity has made great progress as a species, there are many frontiers yet to be explored. Imagination is the tool that enables us to confidently step into the unknown. There are many good books available in the market to stimulate our imaginative thinking process. A good example are the books by [Edward de Bono](#) called "The six thinking hats" and "Lateral Thinking: Creativity step by step".

According to pro cyclist Jamie Paolinetti, "Limitations live on in our minds. But if we use our imagination, our possibilities become endless.". Think of this before we have the tendency to shoot down an idea. Imagine the unimaginable and the endless knowledge of this world will open up to us!

Chapter VIII: One in Seven Billion!

I remember the first day that I had started to search for a job in Mumbai city back in 1998. I had to take a local metro train from a train station called "Kurla" and it would take me to the centre of Mumbai city. I remember the crowd outside the Kurla station being a little like the picture below. The crowd was so huge that it took me at least 20 minutes to get out of the station and onto the main road, which was only 500 metres long. I felt lost in the crowd! It was as though I was an ant, lost among the thousands of other ants scurrying to and fro with various purposes in their minds.

When we wake up every day, we worry about ourselves, our families, what we will do during the day, what we will achieve during the day and what the day has in store for us. The fact is we are one in 7 billion people (rough estimate) in the world today. Each of us have been given the unique opportunity to experience life and make changes in this world. Some big and some small, some good and some bad. Each of us in our daily life with our actions touch other people in many ways that we cannot imagine. Pride really does not have a place when we think of our place in this world as one among the 7 billion, given one chance to live a meaningful life.

The picture alongside is a scene from people trying to board a local train in Mumbai. Too many people with too few resources. Each day is a rat race, a competition for the few resources available. Out of the 7 billion people, there is only a very small percentage of people who are very well off, a large section of middle-class people and a vast majority of poor people. Many people struggle to make ends meet, to get a single meal during the day. There are countries where the scenes at the railway stations are very different, with luxurious coaches and people dressed in extreme fashion. They do not experience the struggle that many people around the world go through, just to stay alive. Life is not fair but that is life. Of course, I am in no way implying that Kurla is a bad place. In fact, Mumbai is a beautiful city, filled with vibrant life. There is never a dull day in Mumbai.

Even while travelling on a crowded train or walking through the crowded station, if we stop to observe, we can see countless acts of kindness being done every day by people. Be it giving alms to the poor, giving your seat to an older person in a crowded train, trying to protect a child from getting hurt on a moving train, giving way for the weak and elderly to board first. In our hustle and bustle, we may not see these acts of kindness. We are taught that it is a cutthroat world out there, you need to be street smart and all else.

One in seven billion! For a moment, if you are worried about events in your life, higher privileges you want, more money, more luxury, take a minute to slow down and be a part of the crowd in a place like Kurla. You will feel humbled. Thank God for all the good things he has given you in your life, all the things that we take for granted and these troubles will feel like nothing. Imagine if we could stop thinking of ourselves for a minute and put ourselves in the place of one of the other people in the crowd to see if there was any way we do help them to make their lives happier. A kind word, a good gesture, a helping hand is all it takes. To start with when we are back at our place of work or study tomorrow, think of one of the persons who are less privileged and serving the company or institution where you work or study. Do we know their names? Even a smile, calling out their name and asking "how they are?" can make a big difference.

We are one in seven billion with an opportunity of a lifetime. Be the change you want to see in the world!

Chapter IX: Petrichor!

Time and tide wait for none!

I am still not over wishing my friends and colleagues a Happy New Year 2020! So, for all my friends, colleagues and readers on LinkedIn whom I could not yet meet in person this year, here's wishing you all a fabulous new year 2020!

Since the beginning of the year, I have been thinking for a while what I should share with my readers. So here are my first thoughts for the year that I would like to share with all of you.

We all know that we have five senses. Sight, Sound, Taste, Smell and Touch. There is also a sixth sense, which is much talked about, i.e. extra sensory perception. There is no doubt about the first five senses of the human body but the sixth sense is quite controversial. I am not sure how we can prove its existence but I have at many times felt that I could feel the presence of someone in a room or someone watching me from afar without actually seeing or hearing them. Is this the sixth sense? I do not know. In any case, the sixth sense is not my topic of discussion today.

What I want to share with you is something I felt is more profound and it relates to the five senses. I would like to think that God has given us these senses to enjoy life and experience the wonders of this beautiful world.

To this end, man has created so many versions of attractions and devices which cater to the sense of Sight, Sound and Taste which we can enjoy sitting in our homes. To be specific, movies, theatre, shows, plays etc. are also attractions which man has made specifically to cater to the sense of sight. We can choose to go online, to theatres, buy discs to entertain our sense of sight, sitting at our homes.

When it comes to taste, there are so many varieties of food which we can experience. You can go to restaurants and buy the choice of your food to entertain your sense of taste. There are Michelin star chefs nowadays who combine the entertainment of taste and sight when it comes to food by preparing and serving beautifully set food items which cater to both sight and taste. All types of food can be prepared and enjoyed at our homes.

When it comes to sound, welcome to the world of music! We all know that we can choose our music from many sources be it online, on our phones, discs, memory cards! Some of us can also make music. There are billboard charts for the best music. Music is celebrated worldwide and this also can be enjoyed sitting at our homes.

Man has created business models and people make tons of money catering to the sense of sight, sound and taste. Man has created mediums through which these three senses can be entertained at our homes.

Here's the thing. There are two senses remaining which have not been catered to as these other three, which is the sense of Smell and Touch.

Let us start with the sense of smell. Although there are several shops where you could go and buy perfumes which cater to your sense of smell, there is yet to be a business model built around fully catering to the human being's sense of smell. For example, if I want to smell the ocean or the recently drenched earth after the rain, I have to travel to the beach or a country where there is rain in abundance to enjoy these smells. Unlike the sense of sound for example, if I want to hear the sound of thunder in the UAE, I could listen to a CD which has this sound recorded. There are so many pleasant smells in this world which is not readily available to human beings as a medium to be bought. What if we built a museum where we could capture all these unique smells and people could visit this place, even people who are not able to see, to enjoy their favorite smells. Or if we invent a device which records the various smells around the world to be enjoyed by us at our homes.

Similarly, if we take the sense of touch, there is no such medium which is available where we could buy and enjoy the various surfaces and objects in this wonderful world God had created. For example, I would love to touch freshly mowed grass, snow, ice bergs and so many things but cannot be done easily unless I physically travel to the place which has these objects or surfaces. So again, what do you think about the idea of creating a museum of various common objects and surfaces where we could go to and enjoy our sense of touch. This would be most enjoyed by people who may be lacking one of more of the other senses for example, people who cannot see or hear.

In our busy lives, many of us do not stop and enjoy this beautiful world God has placed us in, with the five wonderful senses he has given us. So as a starting thought for this year, may we all take a little bit of time out of our busy schedule to see a little more, hear some beautiful sounds, taste some wonderful food, smell some fantastic smells and touch some great things! As we get older, there will be a time when our senses will get weaker and some will fade away. So, let us not take our senses for granted!

By the way, for all who are wondering what is Petrichor, it is the dictionary word for "a pleasant smell that frequently accompanies the first rain after a long period of warm, dry weather." I learnt this new word today, by the way.

About the Author

Bobby Varghese is a senior finance professional with 21 years' experience working in Abu Dhabi, UAE in the Maritime Industry. He holds a Fellow Chartered Accountant's degree from India and a Certified Public Accountant's degree from USA.

Bobby lives with his wife and daughter in the UAE and hails from Kerala, India. He did his schooling in Abu Dhabi India School and later on completed his education in Kerala, India and Mumbai, Maharashtra. He is now back to where he studied after spending around 30 years outside the UAE.

www.ingramcontent.com/pod-product-compliance
Lightning Source LLC
Chambersburg PA
CBHW051927210526
45473CB00006B/2165